DOGS WITH JOBS

Farming Dogs

I0876399

Eric Reeder and Katie Gillespie

MEDIA ENHANCED BOOKS
AV2 BY WEIGL
ADDED VALUE • AUDIO VISUAL
www.av2books.com

Go to **www.av2books.com**, and enter this book's unique code.

BOOK CODE

AVZ84498

AV² by Weigl brings you media enhanced books that support active learning.

AV² provides enriched content that supplements and complements this book. Weigl's AV² books strive to create inspired learning and engage young minds in a total learning experience.

Your AV² Media Enhanced books come alive with...

Audio
Listen to sections of the book read aloud.

Key Words
Study vocabulary, and complete a matching word activity.

Video
Watch informative video clips.

Quizzes
Test your knowledge.

Embedded Weblinks
Gain additional information for research.

Slide Show
View images and captions, and prepare a presentation.

Try This!
Complete activities and hands-on experiments.

... and much, much more!

Published by AV² by Weigl
350 5th Avenue, 59th Floor
New York, NY 10118
Website: www.av2books.com

Copyright © 2020 AV² by Weigl
All rights reserved. No part of this publication may be reproduced, stored in a retrieval system, or transmitted in any form or by any means, electronic, mechanical, photocopying, recording, or otherwise, without the prior written permission of the publisher.

Library of Congress Cataloging-in-Publication Data
Names: Reeder, Eric, author. | Gillespie, Katie, author.
Title: Farming dogs / Eric Reeder and Katie Gillespie.
Description: New York, NY : AV2 by Weigl, [2020] | Series: Dogs with jobs | Audience: Grade 4 to 6. | Includes index.
Identifiers: LCCN 2018053598 (print) | LCCN 2018054184 (ebook) | ISBN 9781489699046 (Multi User Ebook) | ISBN 9781489699053 (Single User Ebook) | ISBN 9781489699022 (hardcover : alk. paper) | ISBN 9781489699039 (softcover : alk. paper)
Subjects: LCSH: Sheep dogs--Juvenile literature. | Herding dogs--Juvenile literature. | Cattle dogs--Juvenile literature. | Livestock protection dogs--Juvenile literature.
Classification: LCC SF428.6 (ebook) | LCC SF428.6 .R44 2020 (print) | DDC 636.737--dc23
LC record available at https://lccn.loc.gov/2018053598

Printed in Guangzhou, China
1 2 3 4 5 6 7 8 9 0 23 22 21 20 19

012019
103118

Editor: Katie Gillespie   Art Director: Terry Paulhus

Weigl acknowledges Getty Images, iStock, and Shutterstock as its primary image suppliers for this title. Every reasonable effort has been made to trace ownership and to obtain permission to reprint copyright material. The publishers would be pleased to have any errors or omissions brought to their attention so that they may be corrected in subsequent printings.

CONTENTS

AV² Book Code 2
Furry Farm Friends 4
Herding History 7
Farming Dogs Today 8
Farm Life 11
Training 12
Hero Dogs 16
Meeting Farming Dogs 19
What Makes a Good Farming Dog? 20
Quiz 22
Key Words/Index 23
Log on to www.av2books.com 24

Furry Farm Friends

What kinds of farm animals can you name? You may think of pigs or horses first, but dogs live and work on farms, too. Farming dogs have many different jobs. Some **herd** other farm animals, keeping them in the right place. Others serve as guard dogs. Farming dogs can also be family companions who protect children. Some of these farming dogs protect **livestock**, such as goats or cows.

Border collies were originally bred to herd sheep. Today, these intelligent dogs are used for a variety of jobs because they are so easy to train.

FACTS UNLEASHED

There are more than 90 different **breeds** of dogs that can work successfully on farms and ranches. Many of these dogs have been bred for this purpose.

Farming dogs develop close relationships with their owners. They work together as a team to get the job done.

Herding History

Farming dogs have been used for a very long time. Today's herding dogs are likely descended, in part, from domesticated dogs that were brought to Great Britain more than 5,000 years ago. These dogs were taken there, along with sheep, in around 3000 BC.

Around the world, other types of farming dogs have been developed. The Catahoula leopard dog was brought to the United States in the 1500s by Spanish explorers. In the 1700s, it was bred and used by French explorers. They used it to find and herd livestock in rough terrain areas, such as forests and mountains.

Over the years, more kinds of farming dogs have been bred. They continue to be used on farms around the world. In the United States, breeds that have been developed include the blue lacy and the popular Australian shepherd.

Farming Dogs Today

Today, many farming dogs live in rural homes, but some live on farms or ranches. They are companions to ranchers and farmers. These dogs do a variety of tasks. They gather and move livestock, such as cows and sheep. It is also their job to watch livestock while the farmers do chores, such as cleaning barns or fixing fences.

Herding dogs need to burn off their high level of energy. If they do not have enough to do, they can become too hyperactive and destroy things. They must have vigorous exercise regularly so this does not happen.

Farm Life

Certain dog breeds are best suited for particular jobs. Border collies and Australian kelpies make good herding dogs. They work on farms or ranches with herds of livestock. These dogs keep the animals together and lead the group where it needs to go. They also fetch animals that have left the herd and bring them back.

The most common breeds of livestock **guardian** dogs are the akbash, Great Pyrenees, and komondor. They independently guard their herd, usually sheep or goats. It is their job to keep the herd safe from predators, such as wolves, foxes, and bears. If the herd is in danger, they let the farmer or rancher know.

Hovawarts are traditional farming dogs. They may guard the farm and the family, pull carts, or act as companion dogs. They can live indoors, outdoors, or both.

FACTS UNLEASHED

Herding dogs lead herd animals from one area to another by barking, biting, and chasing them. These dogs usually lead their herds with the help of a farmer or rancher.

Training

Since farming dogs do a variety of jobs, they have different kinds of training. Herding dogs **instinctively** know some of what they need to do already, but they also have to be taught specific skills. Training helps dogs learn to perform different tasks. Natural instincts, combined with good training and direction, can help make an excellent farming dog.

People who train farming dogs should be able to understand how a dog's mind works. They must be able to see things as the dog does. This may not be the same way humans see them.

Farmers have to expose puppies to livestock. This ensures that they are not afraid. Dogs that are brave, listen well, and are confident make good farming dogs.

Training begins when puppies are young and lasts for several months or longer. Farmers and ranchers teach their dogs **commands**, which must be followed. They also teach the dogs how to do different jobs, such as herding sheep. The farmer will give the dogs commands and let them slowly learn how to herd the sheep. It is important for the farmer to make sure the dogs know when they have done a good job. The farmer must also let the dogs know when they are wrong, so they can change their behavior.

Hero Dogs

Farming dogs do not usually become famous or win awards for their service, but they can help in many brave ways. In North Carolina, a **farmcollie** named Lilly helped keep her owner, Sheryl Chesney, from danger.

Sheryl's pig had given birth to piglets. When she picked up one of the newborn piglets, the mother pig came running toward Sheryl, trying to protect her baby. The mother pig snapped at Sheryl and was going to bite her. Instead, Lilly ran up, snapped at the pig's nose, and backed the angry pig into a corner. This let Sheryl get safely out of the pig pen.

When he was young, Sheryl's husband also owned a hero farmcollie. She kept their farm from being burned down. Someone had been setting buildings on fire all around town. Late one night, the dog noticed a man on the farm who should not have been there. The dog wanted to protect her family and farm, so she knocked the man down, stopping him from setting a fire that night. The man, who had a can of gasoline with him, was responsible for setting the other fires.

Meeting Farming Dogs

Dogs can sense fear and sometimes react negatively to it. This is why it can be dangerous for children to interact with farming dogs. When approaching farming dogs, it is important that children are not afraid, and that they do not run away. For their own safety, children should only approach farming dogs calmly, under the supervision of adults.

FACTS UNLEASHED

Dogs **communicate** in many ways, such as wagging their tails or exposing their bellies. When meeting a new dog, his body language can help you tell if he is calm or stressed.

What Makes a Good Farming Dog?

Many different dog breeds work on farms. Although the requirements for farming dogs may be less specific than for other kinds of working dogs, they do typically have certain key traits. Dogs that herd cattle, for example, should be brave, strong, and hard-working. Herding dogs should also have a high level of energy. A natural instinct to herd farm animals is useful as well. Successful farming dogs will want to please their master, the farmer or rancher, and should be willing to obey commands.

FACTS UNLEASHED

Rat terriers are farming dogs that live indoors. They are close to their owners, serve as watchdogs, and are good with children. Around the farm, rat terriers hunt pests, such as mice, rats, raccoons, and possums.

Quiz

1 How long ago were the first herding dogs brought to Great Britain?

2 Which breed was brought to the United States by Spanish explorers?

3 What can help prevent herding dogs from becoming too hyperactive and destructive?

4 What is another name for farm animals such as cows, sheep, and goats?

5 How long does a farming dog's training last?

6 Which dogs are responsible for protecting a herd?

7 Which farm job is done by border collies?

8 What are Great Pyrenees used for in farming?

9 How do herding dogs lead herds from one area to another?

10 What do rat terriers hunt?

ANSWERS

1 More than 5,000 years ago 2 Catahoula leopard dog 3 Vigorous, regular exercise 4 Livestock 5 Several months or longer 6 Livestock guardian dogs 7 Herding 8 Guarding livestock 9 By barking, biting, and chasing them 10 Pests, such as mice, rats, raccoons, and possums

Key Words

breeds: groups of animals with similar characteristics that are descended from common ancestors

commands: orders given that must be followed

communicate: to share or exchange information

farmcollie: a type of dog covering many different breeds, derived from the original Scotch collie, with traits typical of a good farm dog

guardian: a protector

herd: keep a group of animals together

instinctively: the way animals naturally react

livestock: animals kept on a farm for profit

Index

akbash 11
Australian kelpies 11
Australian shepherd 7

blue lacy 7
border collies 4, 11, 22
breeds 5, 7, 11, 20, 22

Catahoula leopard dog 7, 22
companion dogs 4, 8, 11

domesticated dogs 7

farmcollie 16, 17

Great Britain 7, 22
Great Pyrenees 11, 22

herding 4, 7, 8, 11, 12, 15, 20, 22
Hovawarts 11

jobs 4, 5, 8, 11, 12, 15, 22

komondor 11

livestock 4, 7, 8, 11, 12, 22

North Carolina 16

rat terrier 21, 22

training 4, 12, 15, 22

United States 7, 22

Log on to www.av2books.com

AV² by Weigl brings you media enhanced books that support active learning. Go to www.av2books.com, and enter the special code found on page 2 of this book. You will gain access to enriched and enhanced content that supplements and complements this book. Content includes video, audio, weblinks, quizzes, a slide show, and activities.

AV² Online Navigation

Audio
Listen to sections of the book read aloud.

Book Pages
AV² pages directly correspond to pages in the book.

Video
Watch informative video clips.

Embedded Weblinks
Gain additional information for research.

Key Words
Study vocabulary, and complete a matching word activity.

Try This!
Complete activities and hands-on experiments.

Quizzes
Test your knowledge.

Slide Show
View images and captions, and prepare a presentation.

AV² was built to bridge the gap between print and digital. We encourage you to tell us what you like and what you want to see in the future.

Sign up to be an AV² Ambassador at www.av2books.com/ambassador.

Due to the dynamic nature of the Internet, some of the URLs and activities provided as part of AV² by Weigl may have changed or ceased to exist. AV² by Weigl accepts no responsibility for any such changes. All media enhanced books are regularly monitored to update addresses and sites in a timely manner. Contact AV² by Weigl at 1-866-649-3445 or av2books@weigl.com with any questions, comments, or feedback.